CREATIVE EDUCATION

JACKSONVILLE JAGUARS

JULIE NELSON

Published by Creative Education
123 South Broad Street, Mankato, Minnesota 56001
Creative Education is an imprint of The Creative Company

Designed by Rita Marshall

Photos by: Active Images, Allsport USA, SportsChrome

Copyright © 2001 Creative Education.
International copyrights reserved in all countries.
No part of this book may be reproduced in any form without written
permission from the publisher.
Printed in the United States of America.

Library of Congress Cataloging-in-Publication Data

Nelson, Julie.
Jacksonville Jaguars / by Julie Nelson.
p. cm. — (NFL today)
Summary: Traces the history of the team from its beginnings through 1999.
ISBN 1-58341-046-5

1. Jacksonville Jaguars (Football team)—History—Juvenile literature.
[1. Jacksonville Jaguars (Football team)—History. 2. Football—History.] I. Title.
II. Series: NFL today (Mankato, Minn.)

GV956.J33N45   2000
796.332'64'0975912—dc21   99-015749

First edition

9 8 7 6 5 4 3 2 1

The area around Jacksonville, Florida, has seen its share of historic battles and major changes over the years. Many different flags have flown in the region since the 1500s. The French were the first Europeans to settle along what is now the St. Johns River in northeastern Florida, establishing Fort Caroline there in 1564. That settlement was soon overcome by Spanish armies, who controlled the region for nearly 200 years. The British took over in the 1760s, but Spain reclaimed control after the American Revolution.

Finally, in 1818, a United States army, led by General Andrew Jackson, invaded and captured the territory. Four years

One of the original Jaguars, receiver Ernest Givins.

1995

As a rookie, running back James Stewart led the team with 525 rushing yards.

later, a new town was established near the original site of Fort Caroline. Naturally, the town was named in honor of Andrew Jackson, its newest conqueror, who would go on to be elected President of the United States in 1828.

Since that time, Jacksonville has grown steadily into a major business and commercial center. By the 1990s, Jacksonville was one of the 50 largest cities in the country. It had many outstanding features going for it—fine weather, beautiful nearby beaches, and a strong financial base—but one thing it lacked was a professional sports franchise. Local residents were eager for a new banner to fly over the city—that of a National Football League team.

TOUCHDOWN JACKSONVILLE!

Getting a professional football team onto the field in Jacksonville was a six-year process that began in August 1989 with the formation of a group called "Touchdown Jacksonville!" That group, headed by millionaire businessmen Thomas Petway and J. Wayne Weaver, set out to achieve one goal: to get football fans and business groups in the Jacksonville area interested in bringing an NFL franchise to the city.

The group considered going one of two directions. The first was to persuade an already established NFL team to relocate in Jacksonville. (Leaders of the Jacksonville group had some serious talks about such a move with Bud Adams, owner of the Houston Oilers, but Adams eventually declined.) The second route was to win the rights to a new expansion franchise. After the NFL announced in July 1990 that

Dominant tackle Tony Boselli.

Coach Coughlin's superb leadership made the first-year Jaguars a dangerous team.

it planned to add two new teams by the mid-1990s, "Touchdown Jacksonville!" enthusiastically promoted its city as one of the candidates.

Jacksonville's chances seemed pretty slim, however. Many of the other cities that were candidates were more populous than Jacksonville and could provide a larger market for advertising and ticket sales. In addition, the city's football stadium—the Gator Bowl—was 50 years old and would need to be renovated and expanded.

On October 26, 1994, league owners voted to accept the Carolina Panthers (based in Charlotte, North Carolina) as an expansion team, but they delayed announcing the second city to be selected. One month later, on November 30, Jacksonville got the good news. Beating long odds, the city had been granted the remaining franchise. More than 25,000 fans held a victory celebration inside the Gator Bowl the next day, braving rainy conditions to commemorate Jacksonville's first big win—entry into the NFL.

It had taken more than four years for Jacksonville to earn a place in the league. Now the club would have less than two years to put together a player roster and coaching staff talented enough to compete with the NFL's established teams. That process began in February 1994 with the hiring of Tom Coughlin as the team's first head coach.

A coaching veteran of 25 years, Coughlin had led the Boston College Eagles from 1991 to 1993, turning the team from a loser into one of the nation's top 20 squads. Before that, he had served as an offensive assistant coach for two successful NFL teams—the Green Bay Packers and the New York Giants.

Coughlin was a superb organizer who planned carefully and ran his teams with an iron hand. The opportunity to build a team from scratch in his own way was irresistible. "I wouldn't have done it any other way," said Coughlin, who turned down several other NFL offers before accepting the Jacksonville job. "These days it's imperative to have control of your team's direction and personnel."

Coughlin knew, however, that having control of personnel also meant that he would have a lot of hard work ahead in putting the team together. "Normally a team has one, two, or three major priorities and three to five roster spots to fill," he explained. "We have 53 priorities and roster spots."

Rookie tackle Brian DeMarco helped anchor the right side of the Jaguars' offensive line.

BUILDING THE JAGS

Jacksonville's team—to be known as the "Jaguars"—had three ways to fill those 53 places on its first roster. First, there would be an expansion draft, with each of the league's 28 existing teams making available some of its players for the Jaguars and Carolina Panthers to choose from. These were generally aging veterans or underachievers. Second, the Jaguars would have the first or second pick in each round of the 1995 NFL draft, in which teams would select college players. Third, Jacksonville would have the opportunity to sign free agents who had decided not to re-sign with their former teams and might welcome more playing time or money in Jacksonville.

For nearly a year, Coughlin and his assistants watched college and pro games, interviewed or tried out potential free agents, and decided which kinds of players they wanted to

Versatile running back James Stewart.

Pro-Bowl receiver Keenan McCardell.

1995

Wide receiver Willie Jackson led the Jaguars with 53 receptions and five touchdowns.

select. In February 1995, the team-building process began for real with the expansion draft.

Going into the draft, Coughlin said, "There are two things we have to take care of right away: the quarterback and the defensive-pressure people." With those positions in mind, Coughlin's first 10 draft picks included quarterback Steve Beuerlein, defensive lineman Paul Frase, and linebackers Keith Goganious and Mark Williams. In later rounds, the Jaguars focused on offense, acquiring running backs Le'Shai Maston and Reggie Cobb, receiver Desmond Howard, and tight end Derek Brown.

After the draft, the Jaguars staff sat back to review the talent they had picked up. The most significant acquisition was Beuerlein, a former Notre Dame All-American who had previously quarterbacked the Los Angeles Raiders, Dallas Cowboys, and Arizona Cardinals.

Coughlin and his staff believed that they had secured several other gems as well among the 31 players they selected in the pro expansion draft, particularly on offense. For example, there was Reggie Cobb, who had rushed for more than 1,000 yards for Tampa Bay in 1992; gigantic guard Eugene Chung, who had been a starter for three seasons on the New England Patriots' line before injuries slowed him down in 1994; speedy wide receiver Desmond Howard, a former Heisman Trophy winner at Notre Dame who had never lived up to his potential with the Washington Redskins; and tough tight end Derek Brown, a good blocker and receiver formerly with the New York Giants.

Coughlin wasn't finished, though. In April 1995, he put together the first trade in team history, sending two college draft picks to the Green Bay Packers for Mark Brunell, a young left-handed quarterback. Although Coach Coughlin had planned to make the strong-armed and fleet-footed Brunell a backup to Steve Beuerlein, an injury to Beuerlein would make Brunell the starting quarterback in 1995.

THE ROOKIE AND FREE-AGENT ROUNDUP

The expansion draft was only the first step in finding talent for the new team. During step two—the 1995 NFL draft—Coughlin and his staff continued to focus first on offense. Two of the club's first three picks were mammoth "bookends" Tony Boselli and Brian DeMarco. The two offensive tackles, who weighed a combined 637 pounds, would

Veteran defensive lineman Paul Frase helped the Jaguars net 37 total sacks.

Speedy wide receiver Desmond Howard.

1 9 9 6

Offensive tackle Tony Boselli allowed just three quarterback sacks all season.

be responsible for protecting the Jaguars' quarterbacks and blasting open holes for the Jacksonville runners. "The heart and soul of your football team is the offensive line," Coach Coughlin explained.

The Jacksonville head coach was especially high on Boselli, his first choice and the second pick overall. Boselli was both an athletic and academic All-American at the University of Southern California (USC). "Tony is unique," said Coughlin. "I have a lot of admiration for him not only as a football player but also as a young man. I feel very, very strongly about this pick, and I think the people of Jacksonville will be proud of him."

In addition to the two offensive linemen, Coughlin also used early draft picks to acquire running back James Stewart from the University of Tennessee and quarterback Rob Johnson from USC. Stewart, who had broken most of Tennessee's rushing records, had impressed the Jacksonville staff with his ability to burst through defensive lines and leave tacklers in his wake with his outstanding speed.

After selecting college players through the NFL draft, the Jaguars began exploring the free-agent market. There had been no free agency process in 1976, the last time the NFL had added expansion franchises (Tampa Bay and Seattle). The influx of free agents would help both Jacksonville and Carolina compete much more quickly against veteran teams than did the earlier expansion clubs. While Tampa Bay had gone 0–14 and Seattle had compiled a 2–12 record in 1976, the new Jaguars would win four games, and the Panthers would amaze football experts by recording seven victories in their first year in the league.

Hard-charging halfback Le'Shai Maston.

Middle linebacker Keith Goganious.

Among the top NFL veterans who joined the Jaguars before the 1995 campaign were Jeff Lageman, a six-year starter at defensive end for the New York Jets; defensive tackle Kelvin Pritchett, whose speed and agility had made him one of the Detroit Lions' best pass rushers; offensive lineman Dave Widell, who left Denver to become the Jaguars' first starting center; and offensive tackle Bruce Wilkerson, who had played for eight seasons with the Los Angeles Raiders. One other valuable free-agent signing was rookie placekicker Mike Hollis, who had set an NCAA record by connecting on 68 of 68 points after touchdowns (PATs) in his senior year at the University of Idaho.

Explosive defensive end Tony Brackens finished his rookie year with seven quarterback sacks.

While Coughlin and his assistants were putting together Jacksonville's first roster, the Gator Bowl was being demolished and then rebuilt to meet the guidelines set forth by the NFL. Demolition work began on January 3, 1994. The construction process for the arena—to be named the Jacksonville Municipal Stadium—was laid out in a 20-month timetable, the shortest time period in which a major-league stadium had ever been built in North America.

JAGUARS ON THE PROWL

Amazingly, everything was completed in time for the Jaguars' season opener against the Houston Oilers on September 3. Though the Jaguars would lose the game 10–3, the fact that the new stadium was finished was a major victory in itself. The team would get its first on-field win four weeks later against the same Oilers team. In a rematch in Houston, Brunell led the Jags to a thrilling 17–16 triumph.

The Jaguars defense is one of the NFL's most aggressive (pages 18-19).

Scrambling quarterback Mark Brunell.

strength, and he plays with a mean streak. How good can he be? That's up to him."

Another Jacksonville standout who showed signs of stardom in 1996 was Mark Brunell. The former backup to Packers quarterback Brett Favre led the league in passing with 4,367 yards and 19 touchdowns. He also rushed for more yards than any other signal-caller, becoming the first quarterback to lead the NFL in both categories since the legendary Johnny Unitas did so in 1963. "[Mark has a] physical toughness the other players can rally around," Coughlin said. "There isn't any question in my mind that he's going to improve. He's a great athlete—he's got size, speed, and he's strong and courageous."

The Jaguars let loose a mighty roar in the 1996 playoffs, clawing past Buffalo 30–27 in a first-round Wild Card matchup behind Natrone Means's 175 yards rushing. "We're in this to win," Brunell explained. "We're still hungry. We're not content with what we have. . . . The only way to get any respect is to win."

Jacksonville took another giant step toward respectability the following week, traveling to Denver and capturing one of the most stunning upsets in league history by downing the Broncos 30–27. Means ran for 140 yards, while Brunell shredded the Denver defense with 245 passing yards. It was Denver's first home playoff loss in 12 years and the Jaguars' seventh straight win. Forty thousand Jaguars fans waited at the Jacksonville airport until 1:30 in the morning to welcome their heroes home.

Although Jacksonville's dream season ended the following week with a 20–6 loss to New England, the Jaguars were be-

Linebacker Eddie Robinson was one of Jacksonville's top tacklers, making 161 stops.

1 9 9 8

Starting defensive end Renaldo Wynn contributed 34 tackles in his second NFL season.

ginning to get the respect they deserved. Coughlin was named AFC Coach of the Year, and McCardell became the first Jaguars player elected to the Pro Bowl. Brunell would also travel to Hawaii as a Pro-Bowl alternate but would earn Player of the Game honors after leading the AFC to victory over the National Football Conference's best.

CLIMBING HIGHER

Before the 1996 season, most football fans had recognized Mark Brunell as Jacksonville's rising star. By the end of the season, however, running backs Means and Stewart had combined for 1,230 yards, and receivers McCardell and Jimmy Smith had become one of the best duos in the league, each topping the 1,000-yard mark. The Jaguars had more than one star, and their offensive weaponry would no longer be a secret in 1997.

Before the start of the season, Brunell suffered a painful knee injury that kept him on the sidelines for several weeks. Despite the loss, the Jaguars went 4–0 in the preseason and went into the regular-season opener against the Baltimore Ravens with backup quarterback Rob Johnson at the helm. Though Johnson suffered a leg injury as well, the Jaguars prevailed 28–27.

In the next game, Jacksonville started yet another quarterback—its third one in as many weeks. Tensions were high as Steve Mathews made his first NFL start ahead of his two injured teammates. But the worries were unnecessary, as the inexperienced Mathews looked like a veteran, passing for 252 yards and guiding the Jaguars to new team records for points scored and margin of victory in a 40–13 rout of the New York Giants.

Brunell soon returned to the starting role, and the Jaguars kept rolling. One of the season's top highlights was running back James Stewart's five-touchdown performance in a 38–21 win over Philadelphia on October 12. Stewart, who replaced an injured Means early in the game, became only the fourth player in NFL history to achieve such a feat.

Receivers McCardell and Smith also continued to shine, each recording a second consecutive 1,000-yard season. Despite the fact that the Jacksonville defense was seriously plagued by injuries, particularly along the front line, it allowed an average of fewer than 20 points per game—a new franchise best.

Jacksonville improved its record to 11–5 in 1997 but could not duplicate its playoff success of 1996. Denver got revenge for the previous year's upset, destroying the Jaguars 42–17 in the first round of the playoffs.

Despite the disappointing finish, the Jaguars had accomplished yet another expansion team first: qualifying for the playoffs in two of their first three seasons and improving their overall record to .500 (24–24) in only three years.

Michael Huyghue, senior vice president of Jacksonville football operations, explained the reason for the Jaguars' success. "It's no secret," he said. "We just had a philosophy of building with youth, with young players from the college draft and young free agents. . . . We thought we would try to grow the team on a three-year basis, so that the young players we had could mature to the peaks of their careers in that third year."

Ferocious safety Donovin Darius made 74 defensive stops and forced two fumbles.

One of Jacksonville's brightest stars, halfback Fred Taylor (pages 26-27).

BRUNELL AND TAYLOR: THE BIG CATS

1998

Placekicker Mike Hollis had another outstanding season, making 66 of 71 total kicks.

Jacksonville shuffled its roster a bit before the 1998 season. Natrone Means returned to his old team, the San Diego Chargers, and backup quarterback Rob Johnson was traded to Buffalo in exchange for draft choices. The Jaguars drafted two talented rookies, running back Fred Taylor and safety Donovin Darius, and picked up cornerback Deon Figures through free agency. Jacksonville would again finish with an 11–5 record—good enough to win the AFC Central Division championship.

Although the Jaguars finished with a strong record, it did not come easily. After starting the season 5–0, the team seemed to lose key players to injury almost every week. Running back James Stewart was lost for the season with a knee injury, and an ankle sprain to Brunell cost the Jaguars two potential wins late in the season.

Brunell's value to Jacksonville was clearly demonstrated by his absence. After third-string quarterback Jamie Quinn was forced to assume the starting role, the Jaguars were obliterated 50–10 by the Minnesota Vikings. "He's our heart," McCardell said of Brunell. "He's the piece of the puzzle that can get us to the Super Bowl."

Though the injury to Brunell was costly, the loss of Stewart became less of a problem with the inspired play of rookie running back Fred Taylor. Taylor, a 6-foot and 231-pound first-round draft choice, became the Jaguars' starter early in the season. The speedy young halfback responded to the promotion by dashing for a 52-yard touchdown run on his very first carry.

"You fall asleep for one second playing against someone like Fred Taylor, and, boom, he kills you," said Jaguars defensive tackle John Jurkovic. "That kind of threat puts constant tension on a defense. It's like Chinese water torture. The whole game it's just drip, drip, drip—then, bam, he's gone."

Taylor made the most of his opportunity in 1998, running for 1,223 yards and 14 touchdowns and twice earning AFC Rookie of the Month honors. "What I really want in the next few years is to be considered with the league's elite backs, Terrell [Davis] and Barry [Sanders]," Taylor said. "I wouldn't have said that at the beginning of the season, but now it's not such a bold statement."

Taylor's boldest statement in his first NFL season may have been his performance against the New England Patriots in the first round of the playoffs. Taking handoffs from a limping Brunell, who had just returned to the lineup, Taylor finished with 162 yards to lead Jacksonville to a 25–10 win.

Once again, though, Jacksonville came up short in its run for the Super Bowl, losing 34–24 to the New York Jets. Still, Coach Coughlin was proud of the effort. "We fought our tails off," he said. "It wasn't always pretty. It was dismal at times. But it's a long game, and the courage and the fortitude that these players displayed was just tremendous."

Despite his injury problems, Mark Brunell finished the season with 2,601 passing yards and 20 touchdowns, surpassing the 10,000-yard mark in only his fourth season as an NFL starter. "He's efficient, he makes plays, he's accurate, [and] he can throw the deep ball," explained San Francisco 49ers All-Pro quarterback Steve Young. "That's what you need to have in the NFL to be successful."

1 9 9 9

Cornerback Aaron Beasley picked off six passes, returning two for touchdowns.

Deep-threat receiver Jimmy Smith.

Hard-hitting outside linebacker Kevin Hardy.

Fans expected speedy cornerback Fernando Bryant to emerge as the next Jaguars star.

In 1999, Brunell led the Jaguars to a new level of success. Combining a big-play offense with a swarming defense, Jacksonville cruised to a 14–2 record, the AFC Central crown, and home-field advantage throughout the playoffs.

The Jaguars' first playoff game pitted them against the Miami Dolphins. What was supposed to be a thrilling cross-state matchup quickly turned into one of the biggest routs in NFL playoff history. Jacksonville opened up a 41–7 halftime lead before coasting to a 62–7 win. Fred Taylor began the blowout early with a 90-yard touchdown run—the longest in playoff history.

Jacksonville's opponent in the AFC title game was Tennessee, the team that had handed the Jaguars their only losses of the season. Although the Jaguars scored first, the momentum would not last. As a determined Titans defense blitzed Brunell relentlessly, the Jaguars offense sputtered. Tennessee pulled away to win 33–14.

The loss was a big disappointment to Jaguars fans, but Coach Coughlin saw plenty of reasons for optimism. "I think a lot of good things happened," he said. "The defense was greatly improved. The running game was number one in the league. We continued to develop young players. You're not going to win 15 games without being a pretty good football team."

The Jaguars have enjoyed record levels of success in their first five seasons, making the playoffs four times and reaching the AFC championship game twice. The only step remaining for today's Jaguars is to raise the flag of an NFL champion over the historic city of Jacksonville.

796.332 Nel
Nelson, Julie.
 Jacksonville Jaguars
 99015749